Let's Teach with Bible Games

Let's Teach
with Bible Games

by
Donna Fillmore

BAKER BOOK HOUSE
Grand Rapids, Michigan

This book is dedicated
to my father

Bernard A. Fillmore

who often brightened the day
with a game.

Copyright 1978 by
Beacon Hill Press of Kansas City
Reprinted 1979 by Baker Book House

ISBN: 0-8010-3488-4

First printing, June 1979
Second printing, February 1981
Third printing, December 1983

PHOTOLITHOPRINTED BY CUSHING - MALLOY, INC.
ANN ARBOR, MICHIGAN, UNITED STATES OF AMERICA

Contents

Preface

"A little bit of sugar makes the medicine go down," sang Walt Disney's Mary Poppins. Her point, of course, was that even things which are very distasteful can be made pleasant—in fact, downright fun.

This same principle applies to Christian education. When games are used as a teaching tool, learning Bible facts, verses, and concepts becomes almost painless—both for teachers and pupils. Even very simple devices can help to change learning from routine drudgery to an exciting adventure.

I first became interested in Bible games in 1967 when I was teaching a class of active junior boys. Week after week, I struggled to make the lessons interesting and keep their attention. But by the end of class, I was always worn out.

One week, the Lord gave me a flash of inspiration. "Let's divide up into teams," I suggested. "Team 1 against Team 2." I then proceeded to simply ask the questions from the workbook orally, alternating between the two teams.

The response was enthusiastic. I discovered, moreover, that the boys were much better motivated to listen to the Bible story when they knew their team was counting on them to know something in the game which followed.

Since that time, I have continued to use and enjoy Bible games in Christian education work. It is satisfying to know that learning can be a pleasure, for both pupils and teachers.

In the pages to follow, you will find all sorts of Bible

games. Most of them are simple to make and use. The devices are planned so that the same game can be used over and over simply by changing the questions (or other types of content) covered in the game. Some games require only a supply of questions printed on 3 x 5 cards.

You will also discover (1) why Bible games are an important teaching tool; (2) types of game techniques suitable for use in church-related activities; (3) principles for using games effectively; and—most important—(4) how to make and use again and again different Bible games.

Using Bible games is only one of many effective teaching methods in Christian education. There are times when the content or purpose of a session may make the use of a Bible game inappropriate. But as you read through this book, I hope you will discover, as I have, that under the right conditions, a Bible game is one of the most appealing, challenging, and effective ways of teaching boys and girls —and their teachers too!

Next Sunday, why not surprise your class and say, "Let's play a Bible game!"

—DONNA FILLMORE

1

The Wonderful World of Bible Games

"Let's play a game!" These magic words almost instantly bring a sparkle into the eyes of most boys and girls. Why? Because children love to play games. Listen to them for a short while and sooner or later you will hear the words, "Let's play . . . house . . . jacks . . . baseball . . . Scrabble."

To adults, it may first appear that children are merely having fun when they play games. But look again. Playing "house," for example, helps children to identify with adults in their real-life roles—roles that the children will someday assume.

Jacks or baseball helps children develop physical skills and coordination. Scrabble encourages spelling/vocabulary skills. And almost all games involve children in making choices and accepting the result. *Obviously, children learn through games, even when they are not aware of doing so.*

Not just any game, however, is suitable for use in Christian education. Nor is the fact that "children love games" enough reason to use them for Bible teaching. Our teaching time is limited and precious. We must use it to best advantage in teaching God's Word to boys and girls. *The primary purpose of Bible games is to educate.* There-

A "Books of the Bible" game makes learning fun

fore, in order to be a valid teaching tool at church, a Bible game must do one or more of these things.

- Teach Bible facts and truths
- Review Bible facts and truths
- Develop skills such as (1) using the Bible or Bible research materials; (2) following rules and playing fair; or (3) applying Bible truths to life.
- Aid in Bible memorization and understanding
- Introduce a new topic or unit of study
- Lead into the day's Bible study

In addition to these things, it is important to remember that no Bible game should be an end in itself. While the device needs to be interesting enough to lend excitement to the activity, learning a new game technique is not the reason for playing a Bible game. The game device is only a means to any one of the ends described above. Therefore, Bible games should be simple and easy to learn. The device chosen should easily lend itself to accomplishing the purpose of the game.

The apostle Paul, in speaking of his many-faceted ministry, said, "I have become all things to all men so that by all possible means I might save some" (1 Cor. 9:22, NIV).* Earlier in the passage, he spoke of adapting himself to the Jews, Gentiles, the weak, and the strong. Teachers of boys and girls could easily insert the word "children" in this passage. And in order to win children and help them learn from God's Word, we must use methods that will attract their attention and keep their interest. Enjoying Bible games is one such method.

When a review game is used, the pupils must first learn the Bible material so they can play the game. Devices that teach new material help hold the child's interest and make learning easier for him. Thus, when used correctly, Bible games can help boys and girls not only to learn, review, and apply Bible truths, but to discover that Bible study is both interesting and exciting.

Choosing and Making Bible Games

In the pages to follow, you will find games of all types: Spinner, Sorting, Trail, Toss Board, Matching, and Question-and-Answer, to name just a few. Some games such as Ticktacktoe, Concentration, and Bible Basketball are adaptations of familiar games. Many of the games can be used by individuals, teams, or both.

With so many game types available, the first thing you must do is to choose the one you wish to use on a given occasion. Follow these steps.

---

*From the *New International Version*, copyright © 1973 by the New York Bible Society International. Used by permission.

1. Consider your teaching purpose. Are you trying to teach new material? recall and reinforce what has been learned? develop skills? Before you can select the appropriate game, you must know what you want to accomplish with it.

2. Look through the suggested games and find those which can be used to accomplish your purpose. Each game is labeled to help you know its purpose, and the ways it should be played. Most of the games in this book are suitable for recall/reinforcement. Some can be used to teach new material or develop a skill.

3. Consider the interests and abilities of your pupils. In general, most of these games are suitable for children in grades 1 to 6. For young primaries, however, choose games that are simple and less competitive. If you have a class of boys, Bible Basketball may be most appealing.

4. Check to see what materials you have on hand. Most of the games are very simply made from cardboard, index cards, and felt markers. A few, however, require additional materials. Be sure you have, or can get, the things that are needed.

After you have considered all these factors, choose the game technique that appeals most to you and will fit your need. You are then ready to prepare the game board and other game parts.

Materials for Making Games

With only a few basic supplies, you can create an endless assortment of useful and interesting learning games. Your most expensive purchase will be the felt markers and X-acto knife; but these are well worth the investment.

1. *Watercolor or permanent felt-tip markers* in three sizes—small, medium, and large point. Most discount

houses have inexpensive sets of 10 to 12 colored markers. These usually come in the small and large points. For medium points, you may have to try an office supply house, camera or hobby shop. Test permanent markers on the cardboard or paper you are using for your game. Some markers run on some paper surfaces.

2. *Index cards* in a variety of colors, or construction paper. I prefer index cards because they are stiffer and have a nicer finish. To get a good variety of colors, you will probably have to go to an office supply house. There you can usually get seven or eight different colors, in two sizes—3 x 5 and 4 x 6 inches. If you use white cards, color code them with different colors of felt marker.

3. *An X-acto knife.* Most dime and discount stores carry a large knife that uses razor blades. For smaller, finer work, try to get the X-acto brand knife available at an office supply store or hobby shop. If you cannot get either type of knife, a single-edge razor blade will do.

4. *Letter envelopes* for making pockets. The 3½ x 6¼ inch size works well and comes cheaply in boxes of 100 or so. Or any handy size will do.

5. *Gummed picture hangers,* or screw-in cup hooks. These are great for games which require hangers, such as Concentration, Ticktacktoe, and others.

6. *Cloth or plastic tape* in various colors. If you are making basic games which will be used over and over, this adds a nice decorative touch and helps keep the game from getting bent up. There is also a clear plastic tape which is nice for some purposes. Masking tape is also useful, but much less permanent.

7. *Poster board* in various weights and colors. Discount and dime stores usually carry four or five colors in the lightweight board. For heavier stock, go to a camera, office supply, or hobby shop. Poster board is relatively expensive; but for a permanent game, it is practical and pretty. Use heavy weights alone. Glue lighter weight board on top of corrugated cardboard.

8. *Cardboard* in various sizes and weights. This is your least expensive item. Cut down cardboard boxes; save the inserts from hosiery packages. Use the backs of memo pads in various sizes.

A good basic rectangular size for cardboard is 12¼ x 17½. A good square size is about 15 x 15.

9. *An assortment of plates* in various sizes (for making

14

circles). This is the easiest way to make perfect circles. Just lay the plate, top side down, onto the cardboard and draw around it with a felt marker. Go to a Salvation Army or Goodwill store and purchase these for 10 to 25c each.

10. *Two-pronged paper fasteners* (split pins) and large safety pins. These make the quickest and most useable spinners.

11. *Clear Con-Tact paper* (or a similar brand). If you are making a game for long-term use, this will help preserve it nicely. Use the paper to cover most gameboard surfaces and permanent playing pieces. *Do not use Con-Tact paper on any game surface where you must glue on envelopes or gummed hangers. Glue will not stick to the plastic.*

12. *Rubber cement.* This is the best form of glue for mounting construction paper or poster board onto another surface. For a better bond, coat both surfaces; let dry until tacky, align, and press. Be careful in aligning. If the two glued surfaces touch, they grip tightly and cannot be moved.

13. *White glue.* This is best for gluing on gummed picture hangers. (See details under "Making and Using a Concentration Board.")

14. *A 12-inch ruler, and 36-inch yardstick* in metal, plastic, or wood.

15. *Plasti-Tak and Scotch (cellophane) tape.* Both the single and double-sided are useful.

With these materials, you can make almost every game in this book. A few require some additional inexpensive materials. These are listed with the game.

Developing Questions for Bible Games

Although the various devices described in the following pages lend excitement and fun to Bible games, it is the questions used in the game that determine their effectiveness as teaching tools. When making and using Bible games, therefore, think first of what you want to accomplish with the children. Then pick the game that will best serve this purpose. Remember that Bible games may be used to:

—teach new Bible facts, truths, or verses;

—review previously learned facts, truths, or verses;

—help children develop certain skills or apply Bible truths to life.

Other factors you will want to take into consideration as you plan a Bible game are:

—What are the ages and/or skills of the children?

—What are the session or unit aims I need to consider?

Types of Game Questions

Questions for Bible games fall into two major categories: (1) those designed to teach or review Bible facts, truths, or verses, and (2) those designed to help pupils apply biblical truths and concepts to life. In a few cases, these two groups of questions may overlap slightly.

A Bible review question tests whether the child remembers what he has been taught. The material being tested may be a Bible fact, truth, or verse. For example:

Bible fact: What was the name of Joseph's youngest brother?

Bible truth: True or false—It is all right to cheat on a test if you have been sick and couldn't study.

Bible verse: Jesus said to (love, hate) one another.

The same factual material can be used to teach new

information when color coding or other devices are used to help the child find answers to the question.

Bible application questions encourage the child to use the facts he knows and to apply them to life as skills, or in problem solving. For example, a "sword drill" is an activity in which pupils take the facts they know about Bible books and other divisions, and apply this to the task of finding Bible references. Another type of application question is this: "Tell what you would do if your best friend told a lie about you," or "What Bible verse can you quote when you are afraid?"

Bible truth and Bible application questions are very similar in that they take the child beyond just rote memory of facts and help him to think about principles and applications. However, Bible application questions usually involve the child in a little more complicated reasoning than a Bible truth question.

Both types of questions—those which teach and review, and those which help to apply—have their place in Bible games. Children need to know certain facts in order to draw conclusions; but they need to go beyond just facts to the principles and applications of Christian teachings.

When making up fact questions, however, try to distinguish between important facts and trivia. For example:

Trivial: What kinds of animals did the traders from Egypt ride?

Important: How did Joseph's brothers feel when Jacob gave Joseph a coat of many colors?

Ways of Stating Game Questions

There are many, many ways of stating Bible questions. Here are only a few of the possibilities:

● *True or False*—Joseph did not trust God when he got to Egypt. (False)

17

• *Multiple Choice*—When Potiphar's wife lied about Joseph he was: *(a)* thrown to the lions; *(b)* killed; *(c)* put in jail. *(c)*

• *Missing Word*—Finish this sentence: Jesus said that we must _____ our enemies. (love)

• *Riddles*—I had 11 brothers who hated me. Who am I? (Joseph)

• *Finish the Sentence or Verse*—"I am with thee and will keep thee _____." (in all places)

• *Matching*—(See chapter 6 for ideas.)

• *Who Said It?*—Who said, "Follow me and I will make you fishers of men"? (Jesus)

• *Tell a Bible Verse that Relates*—What Bible verse will help a person who is afraid? (Pupil quotes a verse he has learned.)

• *Paraphrase*—Say this verse in your own words, "What time I am afraid, I will trust in Thee." (Ps. 56:3. The child restates in his own words.)

One of the best sources of questions is the pupil's workbook that goes with your age-level of curriculum materials. In fact, if your pupils dislike a lot of reading-writing activity, you can help them to do their pupil-book activities by means of a game. Here are just a few samples of ways to adapt the materials. Words in italic are those which came right from a pupil book.

True or False: *God helped Moses' parents think of a wise way to save their baby.* (True.) This question came from a printed checklist.

Finish the sentence. *Many years had passed since Joseph came to Egypt. Now there was a new (a)* queen; *(b)* law; *(c)* king. (C.) This question came out of a printed Bible story.

Finish the verse. *"We are labourers* _____ (together with God"). This came from the Bible memory verse.

18

Who Is Trusting? *"Things won't be easy for awhile, but God will help us."* (Trusting.) This question came from a checklist. The teacher could read the brief open-end story to children, then let different players evaluate the various statements in the checklist.

Finish the sentence: *"I can put God first in my life by . . ."* (Pupils give their ideas.) This came from an open-end sentence for pupils to finish in writing.)

Who said, *"I do not know Jesus and I am not one of His followers"?* (Peter) This came from a short story pupils were to mark.

Sources of Game Materials

PICTURES:
    Pupil books and handwork pages
    Story papers
    Visual-aid resource packets
        —Story board figures
        —Small teaching pictures
        —Large teaching pictures

QUESTIONS:
    Stories in the teachers' manuals
    Stories and/or activities in pupil books

Book of Bible questions are available in religious bookstores. These may not be stated in the form you will use for a particular lesson, but they do give good ideas for types of questions and material to cover.

Tips for Using Games Successfully

Although Bible games are an exciting way to teach, they can present problems if not used carefully. One of the biggest problems is in class discipline. It is easy for pupils to become carried away with the fun—or to get into disputes over how the game is to be played.

To prevent these, and other problems, follow simple guidelines for efficient and effective use of Bible-game activities.

1. Be sure that all pupils understand the game rules. If you need to, write the rules on a sheet of paper so players can refer to them as needed.

2. If a game is to be used by a pupil as an individual activity, you will need to write up complete instructions, plus an answer key. In order for a game to be an effective learning tool, the pupil must be able to check his work and correct his errors.

3. If your pupils are poor readers, let a teacher read all of the questions. This speeds the game considerably and helps to keep discipline problems to a minimum. Often when poor readers are struggling to read questions, other pupils become bored and find other ways to occupy their time.

4. In general, follow this plan for asking questions. Ask a question of the player whose turn it is. If he cannot answer, allow the next player or the next one on the opposite team to try to answer. If he fails, read the answer and use the question later. This keeps the game short and prevents a lot of guessing.

5. If the game rules say that any player may try to answer, always give a signal before allowing pupils to raise their hands. Insist that a pupil wait to be recognized before answering. If a pupil yells out the answer, automatically give the point to the opposite team or next player. Do not allow pupils to noisily call out such things as "Call on me," or "I know." Bible games must be kept orderly.

6. Expect a certain amount of excitement and noise,

All children enjoy playing Bible games

but insist on good discipline and fair play. If pupils cannot seem to abide by game or discipline rules you have suggested, stop the game (after fair warning) for that session. Before using it again, remind pupils of correct behavior, and the consequences of failure to follow rules.

7. If you have pupils who come irregularly and were not present when some of the Bible material was taught, team them with pupils who do come regularly. This will save an irregular attender from embarrassment and allow him to enjoy the game. He will also be learning as he plays.

8. With some middlers and juniors it is wise to avoid pitting the boys against the girls. If there is undue competition between sexes, ill will may arise when one team wins the game. On the other hand in some groups, boys and girls enjoy playing against each other and do not seem to

take it personally when the opposite side wins. Do what seems best with your group.

9. Always read the answers to questions pupils miss. In this way the activity aids learning as well as helping recall or reinforce material previously learned.

10. Above all, enjoy the game with the pupils. As you enter into the spirit of the activity with them, you will grow closer to them on a personal level. When the boys and girls discover that you can have fun with them, as well as teach them, they will be more ready to learn from you in other areas.

2

Making and Using
Spinner Games

Making the Spinner Board

Draw a large circle on a piece of cardboard. This is easily done by turning a dinner-sized plate down on the cardboard and tracing around with a felt marker. Divide the circle into sections. It is helpful to have one board with four sections and another with eight for use in various games.

To make the spinner, insert a two-pronged paper fastener (brad) through the end of a large safety pin. Fasten loosely into the cardboard so the pin will turn easily.

Some spinner games call for numbers to aid in scorekeeping. Others use a category system for selecting questions. To make one board do the work of two, put the numbers near the center of the board, keeping them small enough so that a piece of 3 x 3 index card can be attached to each section and still reveal the number.

Spinner Games

Fifty Is Nifty

PREPARATION: On index cards, write questions relating to the current unit of study. On the back of the cards, number at random from 1 to 8. Or, if you have questions of varying difficulty, number them according to difficulty. Place the questions in stacks according to number.

PLAYING THE GAME: Pupils may play as individuals or in teams. Children take turns spinning the spinner and answering questions from the appropriate stack. If a child answers correctly, he receives the card and the number of points shown on it. The first player or team to score 50 points (or any predetermined number) is the winner. If you run out of question cards before the score is reached, jot down the scores thus far, take cards, mix, and use again.

VARIATION: If you want to keep the question cards in the game at all times, choose a teacher or pupil to be scorekeeper. Jot down each pupil's score rather than giving him the question card. Put questions face down at the bottom of the stack after they have been used.

This game is best used to recall Bible facts, truths, and verses. As a group game, let pupils play in teams or let pupils score individually.

Who, What, or Why?

PREPARATION: Use a spinner board with four sections. On a piece of 3 x 3 index card prepare a category label for each section. You will need separate labels for "Who?" "What?" "Why?" and "Spin Again." Fasten a label to each section of the board, using Plasti-Tak so they can be removed later without destroying the board. Make sure the cards do not interfere with the turning of the spinner.

On 3 x 5 cards, write questions based on the current unit of study. Make some questions for each category on the board. On the backs of the cards, write "Who, What, and Why." Stack questions in three piles according to category. Or merely write your questions in a list.

24

PLAYING THE GAME: Pupils may play as individuals or teams. Children take turns spinning the spinner and answering questions from the appropriate category. If desired, use the numbers on the board for scorekeeping. Or you may simply allow 1 point for each correct answer. If a child lands on "Spin Again" he takes a second try.

Use the game for recall of Bible facts, truths, and verses. Play in teams, or let pupils score individually.

Spin-a-Story

PREPARATION: Have ready a spinner board with as many or more sections as you have Bible stories to review. For each story, prepare a 3 x 3 category card with the name of the story on it. Fasten these to the spinner board with Plasti-tak. If you have more spaces than stories, label the leftovers with categories such as "Spin Again," and "Spin for Double Points." Do not have these two categories next to each other.

On 3 x 5 cards or paper, prepare questions about each story. If you use cards, place the questions in stacks according to category.

PLAYING THE GAME: Children take turns spinning the spinner and answering questions from the appropriate category. If a child answers correctly, he keeps the card and scores a point. If not, the card goes to the bottom of the stack in that category. If a child lands on "Spin Again," he takes a second turn. If he lands on "Spin for Double Points," he spins again and receives 2 points for a correct answer to his next question.

VARIATION 1: If desired, use the numbers on the spinner board to keep score. For example, if the story "Good Samaritan" is fastened to section 6 of the circle, the player receives 6 points for a correct answer to his question.

This same game can be played using other categories. Possibilities include:

Spin-a-Name: Use names and questions about Bible characters.

Spin-a-Category: Use mixed categories such as Bible people, Bible places, Bible stories, ideas, events . . . verses.

Spin-a-Verse: Have pupils quote Bible verses or answer questions about them.

VARIATION 2: If you have small pictures to illustrate each story, fasten these to the spinner board in place of name labels. Play the game as you did above, or do this: Have the child give any fact about the story where his spinner lands. Once a fact has been used, it cannot be used again.

What Would You Do?

PREPARATION: Use a board with four sections, or make duplicate cards for a board with six or eight sections. Prepare category cards which say the following: Act out what to do; Tell what to do; Tell a Bible verse that would help; Spin Again. Fasten these to the edge of the spinner circle with Plasti-Tak.

Also prepare some brief open-end situations such as this one. "Jim broke Tom's best airplane. Jim says he is sorry. What should Tom do?"

Keep these stories fairly simple, and related to lesson concepts you have studied recently.

PLAYING THE GAME: Pupils may take turns spinning the spinner. Read a story situation to the player. He must then do what is shown on the spinner circle—act out an ending, tell an ending, or say a Bible verse. If he is acting out an ending, he may choose another child to help him. Scoring is not important in this game.

If a pupil does not know what to do, or does not want to tell, let him "pass." Call on another volunteer to finish the situation.

To make this game even more valuable, discuss with the pupils the ending chosen for the story. Relate what the child said or did to Bible truths you have learned.

Use this game to help pupils relate Bible truths to life.

3

Making and Using a Concentration Board

Concentration is based upon the principle of matching identical, or "go together" material through a process of recall and elimination. The information for Concentration is placed on an even number of game cards. This may be either two identical sets of the same thing, or two different sets of material which match each other in some way. This Concentration board can be used to play a Concentration game. It can also be used for a number of other game activities. For best results the board needs to stand firmly against an easel or metal board.

Making the Concentration Board

Glue an even number of gummed picture hangers (minimum of 16, maximum of 24) to a piece of heavy cardboard. For best results, use Elmer's glue to fasten down the hanger section that has no glue on it. This keeps the hangers from flipping up when you lift off the cards. Arrange the hangers in even rows, making sure you have enough space (vertically and horizontally) between them to hang 3 x 5 cards without overlapping. Allow an extra 2 inches of space below the bottom of the last row of cards.

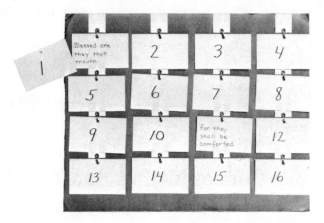

Prepare a permanent set of number cards from 3 x 5 index cards. You need a card for every space on the board. To preserve these, cover the top with clear self-adhesive plastic, such as Con-Tact paper. Punch a hole in the center top of each card. You need to punch a similar hole in all of the game cards you make to use with the Concentration board.

Ways to Use the Concentration Board

There are endless possibilities for playing Concentration. One way is described in detail below. Follow this basic procedure for any of the Concentration variations you wish to use.

Question and Answer Concentration

PREPARATION: Prepare 16 to 24 game cards. On 8 to 12 of the cards, write questions about Bible stories you are studying. On the other 8 to 12 cards write answers to the questions. Both questions and answers should be kept as brief as possible. Punch holes in the cards and mix thoroughly. Hang in random order on the concentration board. Cover with your number cards.

PLAYING THE GAME: Divide the children into two teams, or let them play individually. The first player calls out two numbers on the board. The numbers are removed and the pupil or a teacher reads the material on the cards below. If the cards match—a question and correct answer —the number cards are left off and the player scores a point. He may continue to play until he fails to make a match. If the cards do not match, the number cards are replaced and the next player takes a turn. As players see different cards uncovered, they will eventually recall the locations of matching pairs. The game is finished when all number cards have been removed.

If you want to use Question-and-Answer Concentration to help pupils learn new material, color code the cards in some way. For example, put matched color dots on a question and the answer that matches it. Use a different color (or symbol) for each set of cards. When pupils discover the matching dots, they read the information given on the cards, thus learning something new.

VARIATIONS: Here are only a few of the ways to play Bible Concentration. Players may try to match:

- Pictures to statements about them
- Pictures to Bible verses related to them
- Words with their definitions
- Riddles with answers
- Bible verses to Bible references
- Two identical pictures, statements, or verses. When the match is made, let the child try to quote the verse without looking, tell something about the picture, or read the statements. In this way, you can again play Concentration using material the children have not yet learned. The game thus becomes a learning device.

31

- First halves of Bible verses or Bible statements to last halves of the same.
- A statement or verse with a word missing with the word that completes it.
- Names of Bible characters to facts about them
- Bible characters to statements that character made
- Bible verses to paraphrases of the verses
- Key words from Bible verses to Bible references

Use Concentration to review, or to teach, Bible facts, truths, or verses. Play in teams.

Match the Halves

PREPARATION: Using ideas from the list above, prepare an even number of game cards on 3 x 5 cards. Hang the first half of each pair on the Concentration board, leaving a space beside each card. Mix the other cards and place face down by the board. Number cards are not needed.

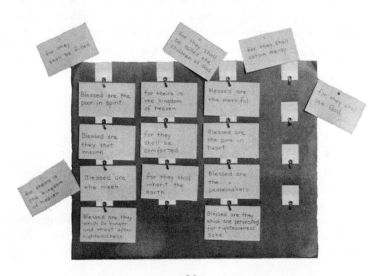

PLAYING THE GAME: Divide players into teams, or let them play individually. The player takes a card from the stack and tries to place it by the card that matches on the board. Score 1 point for each correctly placed card.

This makes an excellent individual activity. Provide an answer key so the pupil can check his work when he finishes. Before he leaves the board, he should remove all answer cards and mix them up again.

You may also use this game to teach new material. Code matching pairs with a colored dot or some other symbol. When pupils match a pair, they read the information on the cards to learn the new information.

Use the game to recall or teach Bible facts, truths, and verses. In a group game, play in teams. Or, use as an individual activity for one pupil.

Match Three

PREPARATION: If your Concentration board has 24 spaces on it, pupils can also enjoy three-part matches. You have room on the board for 8 three-way matches. Use content ideas given previously, but divide the material into three parts. For example, here are some ways to divide Bible verse material:

- Verse, person who said it, reference
- First part of a verse, last part, reference
- First part of a verse, second part, last part and reference
- A verse, the reference, and a paraphrase of the verse
- A verse, reference, picture to illustrate

After you have prepared the cards, put the cards for one part of the match on the Concentration board. For example, hang the verse cards. Place the name cards and reference cards in two stacks, facedown.

PLAYING THE GAME: This is a good individual activity

for one pupil. Follow the rules for two-part matches, except that the pupil must match three parts correctly. Provide an answer key so the child can check his work.

If you wish to play a group game, turn the two stacks of cards face up and lay them out so that all can be seen at the same time. Divide pupils into teams or let them score as individuals. Begin with the first item on the board and let a pupil find the two other cards that match it. If he succeeds, give the score of three points.

If a child places one card correctly, but not the other, award 1 point. Let another child try to find the third matching card to earn a point.

If a child cannot make the correct match at all, let another pupil try. Keep trying until the match is made.

Before playing the game, pupils need to know what they are trying to match (verse, reference, picture; or reference, paraphrase, etc.). It would be helpful to make category cards and Plasti-Tak them to the top of the game board.

As with two-part match, this game can also be used to teach new material if you will code the cards. Scorekeeping is not necessary. Just use the game as a learning activity.

Use this game to review or teach Bible facts, truths, and verses. Play as a group game in teams, or let pupils score individually. Or use for an individual activity.

Take Ten

PREPARATION: Prepare two identical sets of 8 to 12 cards. Number the sets 10, 20, 30, 40, and so on. Use a different color index stock for each set. Place the cards on your concentration board as illustrated.

Prepare questions over a current Bible story or unit of study.

PLAYING THE GAME: Divide pupils into two teams. Alternate between the teams asking your questions. If a team member answers correctly, he may take the lowest number card from his team's side of the concentration board. If he cannot answer, tell the answer and plan to use the question later.

The winner of the game is the team that first removes all cards from their side of the board, or has the highest score at the end of the allotted playing time.

Use to review Bible facts, truths, and verses. Play in teams.

True or False

PREPARATION: This game works well on a Concentration board with 16 or 24 spaces. Print statements on 8 or 12 3 x 5 cards. Some statements should be true; others false. Place the statements in the center of your Concentration board leaving an even number of empty spaces on either side.

PLAYING THE GAME: Let pupils take turns reading a statement and deciding if it is true or false. True state-

35

ments should be placed on the left side of the board; false statements on the right. If desired, score a point for each correctly placed statement. If a pupil places a statement incorrectly, tell why it was wrong; then put it back in the center of the board for another pupil to use later.

If you are using this game with younger pupils, eliminate the scoring. Pupils will enjoy the game just for the opportunity to manipulate the cards. If a pupil misses a card, let the class help him change his decision—then let him put the card in the right place.

This game makes an excellent individual activity. Simply provide an answer key so the pupil can check his work when finished. Before leaving the game, the pupil should replace the statement cards back in the center of the board.

VARIATION: Print Bible verses on the cards, making two cards for each verse. On one card print the verse incorrectly. On the other, print it exactly right. Play as described above.

Use these games to review Bible facts, truths, and verses. Play in teams, or use as an individual activity.

Bible Verse Turn-over

PREPARATION: Make 10 number cards numbered 10, 20, 30 . . . up to 100. (If your concentration board has only 16 spaces, make 8 cards numbered to 80.) Divide each Bible verse you want to review into 10 (or 8) parts, making the reference one of the parts. Write one word or phrase of the verse on each of 10 (or 8) cards.

Place the number cards on the board as shown. Below them place your verse cards, face down. Below the 100-point card place the Bible reference. Below 90 place the first word or phrase of the verse. Follow with the next word or phrase, and so on.

PLAYING THE GAME: The object of the game is for a pupil to try to say the verse with only a few clues showing. Divide pupils into teams or let them play as individuals. Turn over the card with the Bible reference. If the player can quote the verse he receives 100 points. If not, turn over the next card and let another player or team take a try. Continue turning over the cards until someone says the verse correctly. Award that person the number of points shown above the card you last turned over.

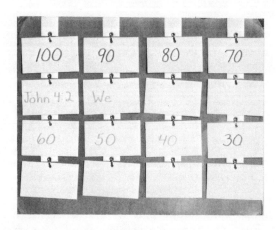

When a verse has been quoted correctly, remove all those verse cards and put a second verse in place. Leave point cards in place at all times.

Use this game to review Bible verses previously learned.

Truth Detector

PREPARATION: This game is good when you have studied a number of Bible characters. For each character you want to review, print three name labels on 3 x 5 index

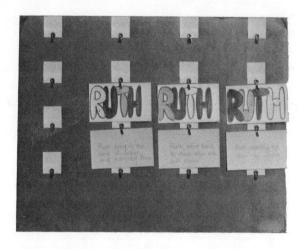

cards. On three additional cards print three statements. Two statements should be false, one true. Make several sets of cards and punch holes in all of them.

Hang the three identical name labels on three spaces of your concentration board. Hang the matching statements below them.

PLAYING THE GAME: This can be used as a low competition game that pupils play as individuals rather than teams. Read the three statements about your character. The player whose turn it is must decide which statement is the true one. If he answers correctly, he receives the true statement card to keep. If not, let the next player try.

After each clue is guessed, place another set of cards on top of those still on the board and continue the game. The pupil with the most cards at the end wins.

For a more competitive game, divide pupils into two teams. Read the three clues—then give a signal. The first person to raise his hand and be recognized may try to answer and score for his team. Be sure, however, that pupils wait for your signal before answering. If a pupil answers out of turn, automatically award the card to the opposite team.

VARIATION: Instead of using three clues about the same person, you may use clues about three different characters. As before, two of the clues will be wrong; one will be right. Pupils must guess which. With this game, you can use some of the same name cards over and over; just change the clue cards from time to time.

4

Making and Using
Ticktacktoe Games

Making the Ticktacktoe Board

Have ready two pieces of heavy cardboard, 15 inches square. Divide one of the boards into nine equal sections. Fasten a gummed picture hanger in each section, leaving space to hang a card 3 x 3. This is the playing side of the game board.

For the other side of the board, provide 5 letter-sized envelopes (at least 3½ x 6¼). Glue the flaps shut and cut the envelopes in half. Glue the halves, open side up, in nine positions on the board to match your playing board. To keep from fastening the pockets too tightly, insert your fingers in them as you glue them to the board. Number the pockets 1 to 9 for easy reference.

Prepare a supply of **X** and **O** markers by cutting index cards to 3 x 3 size. To preserve the cards, cover with self-adhesive clear plastic. Punch a hole in each card.

Tape one edge of each of the boards together, like a hinge, using plastic or cloth tape. The boards will now stand alone.

Use the Ticktacktoe board to review Bible facts, truths, and verses. Play in teams or as an individual activity as described.

Games Using the Ticktacktoe Board

Bible Ticktacktoe

PREPARATION: On 3 x 5 cards, write questions covering material in the current unit of study. Insert one or two questions in each pocket of the game board. Have ready the X and O markers.

PLAYING THE GAME: Divide the children into two teams. The first player on a team calls out the pocket number from which he wants to answer a question. If he answers correctly, place his team marker in this position on the playing side of the board. If he fails, a member of the opposite team may try for the question. If no one succeeds, read the answer and replace the question in its pocket. The first team to score three in a row horizontally, vertically, or diagonally wins the game.

VARIATIONS: For seasonal interest, use different types of game markers. For example, at Christmas time, cut team markers in shapes of stars and bells instead of Xs and Os. At Easter, use crosses and lilies.

41

Pocket Match

PREPARATION: On 3 x 5 cards, write nine statements covering Bible facts, verses, or concepts from the current unit. On nine 3 x 3 cards, write information which completes or matches these cards. Hang the 3 x 3 cards on the playing side of the board. Place the 3 x 5 cards in the pockets, but in different positions from the 3 x 3 cards.

PLAYING THE GAME: This can be used as either an individual activity or a group game. A child chooses a card from the pocket side of the game board and tries to match it to a card on the playing side. When he finds the proper match, he removes both cards from the board and lays them together. Score a point for each correct match.

VARIATION: If desired, punch holes in the 3 x 5 cards and hang them on top of the 3 x 3 cards they match.

Take a Guess

PREPARATION: On nine 3 x 5 cards, write questions based on the current unit of study. Place these in the pocket side of your board.

Punch holes in ten 3 x 5 cards. On nine cards, write the answers to your nine questions. On the tenth card, write "Take a Guess." Cover the "Take a Guess" card with clear, self-adhesive plastic.

Place the nine answer cards in mixed order on the hooks of the gameboard. Cover one answer card with the "Take a Guess" card. Be sure you know which answer is under "Take a Guess."

PLAYING THE GAME: Divide players into two teams, or let children play individually.

The teacher will ask the questions one by one in order. The children, in turn, try to find the card with the correct answer. If the child succeeds, give him the answer card.

If he is wrong, inform him, but do not give the right answer. Go to the next player and use the same question. If the child cannot find the answer to the question, he may say, "Take a Guess." This answer should be revealed only if the child is correct, however.

NOTE: Be sure to explain to children that the numbers in the pockets of your game board have nothing to do with this game or the locations of cards on the playing side of the board.

5

Making and Using
Toss Boards

Making Your Toss Board

Divide a piece of construction paper or poster board
in one of the ways illustrated. Be sure to make each space
large enough to hold category cards. Glue the game board
in the bottom of a shallow box. This will keep buttons or
coins from falling off the board.

*Use toss board games to review Bible facts, truths, or
verses. Let the pupils score individually or by teams.*

Using the Toss Board

Button Toss

PREPARATION: Have ready a large button for each team
or player. Write questions covering the current unit of
study.

PLAYING THE GAME: Divide pupils into teams, or let
them play individually. Set a point or time limit to the
game. Choose someone to keep score for the game.

Alternating between players or teams, ask the pupils
questions. If a pupil answers correctly, let him throw his
button onto the game board. The area where the button
lands determines the number of points the player will
receive.

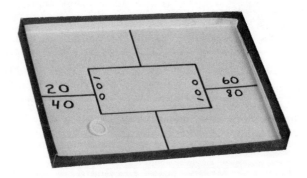

If a player answers incorrectly, give the answer to the question. Plan to use the question later.

VARIATION: If you have questions of varying difficulty, number them, in order of increasing difficulty, to match the numbers on your game board. Have the pupils throw the button before answering a question. The number where the button lands indicates both the question he will be asked and the points he will receive for a correct answer.

If you do not want to use a scorekeeper, do this: Cut index cards or construction paper into small pieces. On each piece write one of the numbers shown on your toss board. Make a half dozen number cards for each number. Put each different number in a small box. When a pupil receives a certain point in the game, he should draw one of the number cards from the appropriate box. At the end of the game, each pupil may add his score from the number cards.

Toss-a-Category

PREPARATION: On small size cards prepare category labels to go in each space of your game board. Fasten the cards to the board with Plasti-Tak. Use the categories suggested under "Spin-a-Story" (chapter 2) or others you wish to use.

Make up questions to fit the categories you have chosen.

PLAYING THE GAME: Pupils, in turn, toss the button onto the toss board. The space where the button lands indicates the category from which the pupil must answer a question. If he answers correctly, he receives the number of points shown on that area of the board.

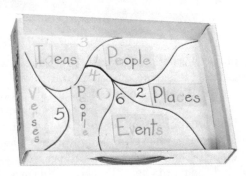

Egg Carton Toss

PREPARATION: Cut off the top and flap from an egg carton. Number the bottom sections of the carton with the numbers 2, 3, and 4. Glue the bottom of the carton into a shallow box or box lid. Number "1" in the bottom of the box lid.

Prepare questions of varying difficulty on 3 x 5 index cards. On the backs number the cards 1, 2, 3, or 4 to match the numbers on the game board. Place the questions in stacks according to numbers. Provide a button or coin.

PLAYING THE GAME: Divide pupils into teams or let them score as individuals. Players take turns tossing a button into the toss board. The number on which the

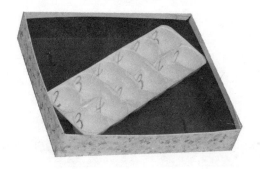

button lands determines which group of cards from which the player must try to answer a question. If he succeeds, he earns the number of points shown on the toss board. If not, give the answer and let the next player take his turn.

Each time a pupil answers correctly, give him the question card to keep score. The game ends when all cards are gone.

VARIATION: For a longer game, reuse the questions instead of giving them to players. Appoint a scorekeeper to keep track of each player's score. Play the game until one player or team receives a predetermined score.

6

Making and Using
Match-up Boards

Making the Match-up Board

This board is the simplest of all to make. Simply find a piece of cardboard large enough to hold several 4 x 6 cards in two columns. You will also need a quantity of wooden or plastic spring-type clothespins. Title the board if desired.

Match-up Games

All match-up games are basically the same and can be played in any of the ways listed in the section about Concentration. One game is described below. Use your imagination to create others.

Match Verses

PREPARATION: On 4 x 6 cards, make two game cards for each verse you want to include. On one card, write the first half of the verse. On the second card write the last half of the verse and the reference. With clothespins, fasten the first halves in a column on the lefthand side of your game board. Fasten the last halves on the righthand side, but in scrambled order.

PLAYING THE GAME: A child may individually rearrange

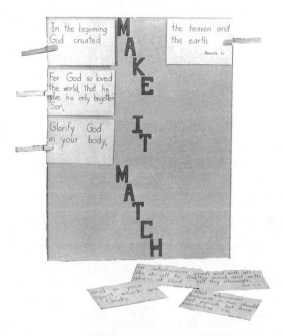

the last halves of the verses so that they match the first halves.

If you are playing in teams, have the first player on a team try to correctly match the first verse on the board. If he can do so, he scores a point for his team. If not, the first player on the other team takes a turn. Keep going back and forth between teams until someone makes the correct match. Then proceed to the second verse.

VARIATION: Instead of placing all cards on the board, place only the first halves, or the last halves. Mix other cards and place facedown in a stack. The player must draw a card and try to match it correctly.

Use match-up games to review Bible facts, truths, and verses. If you have color-code cards, they can be used to teach new material.

7

Additional Games
and Game Boards

Square Off

PREPARATION: Make a game board as illustrated. The easiest way to place the numbers is to cut them from an old calendar and glue them on. Cover the top of the board with clear, self-adhesive Con-Tact paper. (*Note:* If you

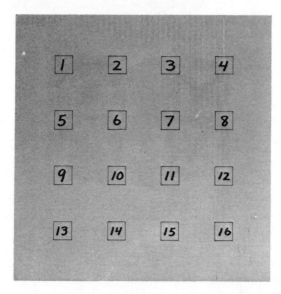

use another brand, check to see that crayon marks will wipe off satisfactorily with Kleenex. Some brands do not.)

Make up a supply of questions based on the current unit of study.

PLAYING THE GAME: The object of this game is to connect four boxes to make a large square. The team or person who *completes* the box claims it with his mark—a crayoned X or O. Players will want to be wary of making the third line in a box since the opposite team might then finish it and claim it.

Ask questions of players or teams in turn. If a player can answer the question correctly, he calls out the numbers of the two boxes (any two, horizontally or vertically) he wishes to connect (with a crayon). If he does not answer correctly, the first player on the opposite team gets a chance at the question. If no one can answer, give it yourself and plan to use the question again later. The team with the most boxes claimed at the end of the game wins.

Use the game to review Bible facts, truths or verses. Play in teams.

Bible Basketball

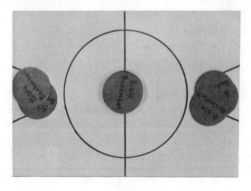

PREPARATION: Prepare a game board as illustrated, using heavy cardboard. From brown construction paper or wrapping paper cut a large quantity of circles and mark them to look like basketballs. Place the stack of "basketballs" in the center of your game board. On a separate sheet of paper, write questions covering material from your unit of study.

PLAYING THE GAME: Divide the children into two teams. Assign each team a basket on the game board. The first player on a team will try to answer the question. If he does so correctly, he places a basketball on his team's basket. If not, give a member of the other team a chance to answer and get a "basket." If that person misses, call a "jump ball." The first person on either team to raise his hand after a given signal may answer the question and claim the basket for his team. Score two points for each basketball in a team's basket.

Use Bible Basketball to review Bible facts, truths, and verses. Play in teams.

Push Button

PREPARATION: On cardboard prepare the game board as shown and label the sections. Provide two pushers (a wooden ruler is good) and two buttons, beans, or coins.

On 3 x 5 cards prepare a supply of questions for each category on the board. Use different colored cards for each category, if desired. Assign a point value to each card at random, or based on the hardness of the question. Put cards in a stack. (*Note:* If you did not use different colored cards for the categories, separate cards by category.)

PLAYING THE GAME: Seat players at opposite ends of the game board. Give each team a pusher and button. The player puts his button on the starting line and pushes with his pusher. In order to count, the button must cross

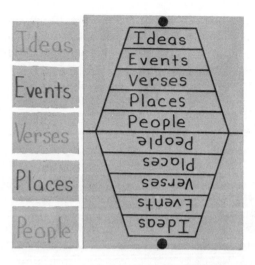

the center line and land in a category. He then answers a question from the category. If he answers correctly, he scores for his team. Allow players to keep the cards when they score.

VARIATION: If you have a limited number of questions and several players, prepare number cards (described under toss board games) and let players draw numbers equal to their scores.

100-Yard Dash

PREPARATION: On heavy cardboard, prepare the game board as illustrated. Write up at least 20 questions for the game. Provide a button or other type of marker for each player on team.

PLAYING THE GAME: The object of this game is for the player to see how many "yards" he can cover on the game board before he misses a question. The teacher will draw a question from the stack and ask. If the player answers correctly, he places his marker on the 10-yard line. The teacher asks another question and the process is repeated. The player keeps going until he misses a question. He must then stay where he is and the second player begins to play.

If a player runs the whole 100 yards in one turn, he retires. Retired players may take turns asking questions of players still in the game.

VARIATION: The game as described above is best for competitive older children (junior age). For younger children who would find it hard to wait their turn, limit the number of questions a pupil may answer in any one turn to three.

Use this game to review Bible facts, truths, or verses. Pupils may score individually or in teams.

How Far Can You Jump?

PREPARATION: On 3 x 5 cards, prepare three groups of questions—easy, harder, and hardest. On the same side of the card as the question write "One Jump" on the easy questions, "Two Jumps" on the harder ones, and "Three Jumps" on the hardest ones. Mix the cards thoroughly and place in a stack facedown. Provide a marker for each player.

PLAYING THE GAME: Let pupils play as individuals. The first pupil takes a card and tries to answer the question. If he answers correctly, he moves up the board the number of spaces shown on the card—one jump, two jumps, or three jumps.

If he answers incorrectly, give the answer yourself. Then let another player take a turn.

Each time a player answers a question, or you give the answer, put the card on the bottom of the stack. Continue the game until one player reaches the end of the board.

Use this game to review Bible facts, truths, or verses. Pupils may score individually.

Picture Hunt

PREPARATION: Prepare the game board from two pieces of cardboard 12½ x 17. Starting an inch from the top of one board, measure off an area 14 x 10½. Cut out this area carefully with an X-acto knife or razor blade. Trim this 14 x 10½ piece slightly (about ⅛ on each side) and cut into 12 equal squares (about 3½ inches square).

In the center of each square, put a generous dot of Elmer's glue. Push a marble into the glue. Allow to dry thoroughly (at least 24 hours). Each piece now has an easy lift-off handle. Number the pieces 1 to 12.

Stack several large teaching pictures on the uncut piece of cardboard. Cover with the cardboard frame which was left when you took out your center piece. Tape the cardboards together on the two sides and bottom with

cloth or plastic tape. Remove all the pictures except the one you want to use for the game.

To make pictures easier to insert and remove, cut out a small notch from the center top of the back cardboard.

Fasten the 12 small squares back into the picture frame to cover the picture you are using. If you use a small piece of Plasti-Tak on each square, they will stay in place even after some squares are removed. For this game, use a picture the children have not seen before.

Prepare 12 questions and number these 1 to 12. Give harder questions higher point values, if desired.

PLAYING THE GAME: Tell the children there is a mystery picture under the cardboard squares. They can reveal it by correctly answering questions. The picture shows a person they will be studying about today.

Let players in turn choose a number. Ask the question that goes with the number. If a child answers correctly, remove the square and give it to him for score-keeping, whatever its point value. If not, let another player have a try. Keep going until all squares are removed to display the picture for the day. The team or individual with the most points wins.

VARIATION 1: Instead of a new picture, use one the children have seen before. Try to see how quickly the children can identify the picture. After each square is removed, let the child try to identify the picture. The child who can is the winner.

VARIATION 2: For a team game, divide the class into two groups. Assign the top six squares to team 1; the bottom six to team 2. Alternate questions between teams. The first team to uncover its half of the picture wins.

Bible Verse Flip

PREPARATION: Cut a piece of poster board or light-weight cardboard to 22½ x 3½ inches. Lay four 3 x 5 cards on the strip so they are even with the top of the cardboard. Allowing an even amount of space between the cards, and along each edge, trace lightly around the cards with a pencil. Punch a hole in the center of each marked area, about a half inch from the top line.

For each Bible verse you plan to use, prepare four 3 x 5 index cards. Punch a hole in the top of each card so they will match the holes on the game board.

Divide the words of each verse into four parts. Include the reference with the last part. Or, if you prefer, divide the verse into three parts and make the reference the fourth part.

Scramble all the cards of each section thoroughly, but do not mix the cards of any two sections. Fasten the groups of cards in order on your cardboard, using small plastic or metal rings.

PLAYING THE GAME: This game makes a good individual activity, or may be used in the large group. In individual activity, the child turns the cards until he finds four that match. Provide an answer key or Bible so he can check his work.

If your children like team competition, make two game boards and place on them identical Bible material. Let a player from each team try to put together a verse. The winner is the first one to correctly finish a verse.

VARIATIONS: If desired, the game board can be made with five or more sections. For each additional section, add 5½ inches to the length of the board. The width remains the same. Position the holes as you did for the first four cards.

Birds in a Tree

Even gummed stickers, such as you can purchase in a dime store (the new pressure sensitive ones are especially nice), can be put to work in a Bible game. One such game is described below. However, the possible variations are endless—limited only by the types of stickers available to you.

PREPARATION: From construction paper cut out two large tree shapes. Use black or brown paper for the stem; green for the leafy upper part. To make the game board more durable, cover with clear Con-Tact paper.

Glue gummed stickers of birds to index card stock. Cover with Con-Tact paper and cut them out. If the birds are rather small, just cut out an irregular shape around the bird rather than trying to cut minutely around it. Put a piece of magnetic tape on the back of each bird sticker.

PLAYING THE GAME: Place your tree shapes on a metal board. Divide pupils into two teams. Alternate between

teams as you ask the questions. Each time a pupil answers correctly, he may take a bird sticker and fasten it to his team's tree. The team with the most birds in its tree wins the game.

VARIATION: For individual scoring in the game, cut out a small tree for each pupil. Prepare bird stickers as before but do not put magnetic tape on the back. Let pupils each try to fill their trees with birds.

This game can be varied in many ways. Here are some possibilities using stickers generally available from your publishing house, dime store, or card and gift stores.

Bees in a Hive—Draw a hive shape on construction paper and use stickers of bees.

Go Fishing—Provide a construction paper "net" and let pupils fill with fish seals.

Flower Garden—On brown construction paper draw furrows as in a garden. Pupils add flower seals.

Fall Fantastic—On construction paper, glue the shape of a tree with bare limbs. Let pupils add colored leaf seals to the limbs and on the ground around.

All of the sticker games can be used to review Bible facts, truths, and verses.

Pick a Flower

PREPARATION: On construction paper (12 x 18 size) draw black lines to represent garden furrows. Cover the sheet with Con-Tact paper. Place it on the metal board and fill each row with prepared gummed sticker flowers.

PLAYING THE GAME: This game works in reverse of the games above. Let pupils play as individuals or in teams. Each time a pupil answers a question correctly, he may "pick" a flower from the garden. The pupil or team with the most flowers is the winner.

Ruler Relay

PREPARATION: Print about 20 questions on separate 4 x 6 index cards. You may use some questions twice, if needed. Or use the same question, but phrase it a little differently each time.

PLAYING THE GAME: Tape a yardstick to the wall. Divide pupils into two teams, and assign each team one side of the yardstick. Alternate between teams asking questions covering the unit of study. Each time a player answers a question, he may take the question card and Plasti-Tak it in place on his team's side of the yardstick. The first team to answer nine questions (or any set number) correctly is the winner.

If the teams are closely matched (neither having missed a question) use a playoff question or two to determine the winner. If you are still tied when all questions are used, declare both teams to be winners.

Measure Your Progress

PREPARATION: On a large piece of cardboard draw two giant-size rulers. Make the spaces on them about 2 inches apart. Mark lines for quarter, half, three-fourths, and one-inch measures. Number the "inches" from 1 to 12. Keep numbers close to left edge so they will not be covered up when construction paper squares are added. Label the rulers Team 1 and Team 2.

From construction paper, cut pieces that are 2 inches by 1½ inches. Use a variety of colors.

Cover both sides with clear Con-Tact paper.

PLAYING THE GAME: Divide pupils into two teams and assign each team a "ruler." Alternate between teams as you ask questions over material pupils have studied. When

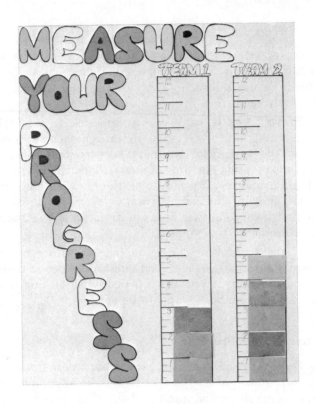

a player answers a question correctly, he may add a colored square to his team's ruler. See which team can measure the most progress.

Use all these games to review Bible facts, truths, and verses.

8

Games Which Do Not Require Game Boards

All of the following games may be used to review Bible facts, truths and verses. They are all group games in which pupils can score either individually or by teams.

Jump over the Fence

PREPARATION: Print questions related to the current unit of study on 3 x 5 cards, or have them on a list. Divide the class into two equal teams.

PLAYING THE GAME: Ask the children questions, alternating between the two teams. If a child answers his question incorrectly, he must "jump over the fence" and join the other team. At the end of the game, the team with the most members wins.

Keep Talking

PREPARATION: Prepare questions covering the current unit of study. For each member of the class, print a 3 x 5 card with his name. Print one additional card which says "Keep Talking." Place these facedown in a stack.

PLAYING THE GAME: Draw the top card from the name card stack and ask this person a question. If he answers correctly, he scores a point and draws the next card, which tells who will answer the next question. If he answers incorrectly, he does not score a point, but draws the next name card. This person will try to answer the same question, then draw the card for the next player.

If a player draws the "Keep Talking" card, he keeps on answering questions until he misses. (Even if a player missed his previous question, he may use the "Keep Talking" card.) After each card is used, place it on the bottom of the stack.

Which Story?

PREPARATION: Prepare title cards for several current Bible stories. On other 3 x 5 cards write two or three question clues about each story. For example, "Which story tells about a young boy who killed a huge giant?" Or, "Which story shows us how important it is to trust God, even when we are afraid?" Or, "Which story does this verse go with (give verse) . . . ?" Lay the title cards on a table, faceup, or place in a sentence strip holder. Mix the clue cards from all the stories and place in a stack, facedown.

PLAYING THE GAME: This game may be played by pupils as an individual activity, or use as a group or team game.

A player takes a card from the stack and tries to place

64

it under the correct story title card. If teams are playing, alternate players between the two teams. If a player places a card incorrectly, a player from the opposite team may try to place it. Score one point for each correctly placed card.

VARIATION: Let children match clues about Bible people with name cards.

Right-O, Wrong-O

PREPARATION: With construction paper or patterned Con-Tact paper, cover two boxes (oatmeal or shoe boxes are good). Label one box "Right-O" and the other "Wrong-O." On 3 x 5 cards, write statements based on the current unit of study. Some of the statements should be true, others false. Place in a stack facedown.

PLAYING THE GAME: Children go through the statements one by one, and place them in the proper box. This game may be played by an individual or group. Players receive 1 point for each correct answer and minus 1 for every wrong answer.

VARIATION: To use this game in the large group, distribute all the statements among players. Players will come up one by one, read their statement, and place it in the proper box. For nonreaders, the teacher may read the statement before the student puts it in a box.

Spell-a-Name

PREPARATION: Choose a Bible character or a key word from the unit you are studying. Prepare two index cards for each letter of the word. Lay these, facedown (in two groups), by letter so that the word is correctly spelled starting with the top card. Also prepare a set of questions about the character whose name is on the cards, or questions over other material in the unit. Be sure to have at least two questions for every letter in the word on your cards.

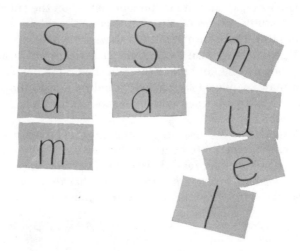

PLAYING THE GAME: Divide the children into teams. Ask questions of the children, alternating between teams. If a child answers correctly, he may turn over the first letter card of his team's word. The first team to spell the word is the winner. If you use all your questions but still have not spelled the word, mix them and use over.

Who's Got the Bowl?

PREPARATION: Have ready a bowl (plastic) that is large enough to hold 3 x 5 index cards. Also have a quantity of questions based on the current unit of study. Place the questions facedown in the bowl. Seat the children in a circle.

PLAYING THE GAME: Sing or play a simple tune while the children pass the bowl from player to player. When the music stops, the person holding the bowl draws out a question and tries to answer. If he answers correctly, he keeps the card and scores a point. If he misses, he puts the card back in the bowl underneath the others. The player with the most cards wins the game.

VARIATION: For a team game, use two circles and two bowls of cards. Teams pass their bowls of cards simultaneously. When the music stops, they each take a card and try to answer. Follow the rules above for scoring. The team with the most cards wins.

Thumbs Up, Thumbs Down

PREPARATION: Make up a number of true-false statements about the current unit of study. These may be statements about Bible facts, or statements that describe right and wrong Christian concepts. For example, "When a person has been unkind to someone, a Christian will try to get even with him."

PLAYING THE GAME: Divide the pupils into teams. Appoint one pupil or teacher to be a scorekeeper. (This person can help count responses.) Then give these signals.

Eyes Closed: Pupils must all shut their eyes.

Question: Teacher will read a true-false statement.

Thumbs Up—Thumbs Down: All pupils on both teams put their thumbs up if they think the statement is true. They put their thumbs down if they think the statement is false. While pupils' eyes are still shut, quickly count the number of right responses on each team.

Eyes Open: Pupils relax their hands and open their eyes. Tell them the correct answer and how many points they earned. The team with the most points wins.

Puppet Play

This game is good when you have several different Bible characters to review.

PREPARATION: Find in your story board files figures of a Bible man and a Bible woman. If your unit has also included children, also find a figure of a child. Using these as patterns, make several copies on plain light-colored

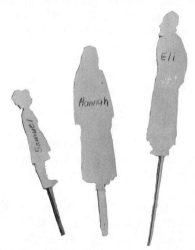

construction paper. Do not draw in face and features—just make silhouettes. Before you cut out the figures, cover the front with clear Con-Tact paper (or any erasable brand).

Cut out the figures and attach a straw or Popsicle stick to the back. Make a puppet for every character in your unit of study. With crayon, write the name of the puppet on the plastic-coated side.

On 3 x 5 cards, prepare an even number of questions or riddles about each puppet. (*Question:* "Who did Gideon and his small army fight against?" *Riddle:* "I won a big battle with only 300 soldiers. Who am I?")

PLAYING THE GAME: Draw question cards one by one and ask the questions. The pupil who has the puppet that matches the riddle or question should hold up his puppet. If he is correct, give him the question card to keep.

If a pupil does not know the answer, or answers incorrectly, give the answer yourself and put the question card at the bottom of the stack. Keep playing until all questions have been answered. Since you have prepared an even number of questions, no one is the "winner." However, pupils will have fun playing the game. This is a good game for younger, less competitive children.

VARIATION 1: For a more competitive game, do this. If a pupil cannot give the answer, or answers incorrectly, give another player a chance to tell which person is described in the question. If that player is correct, he may take the question card and score a point. The player with the most cards at the end of the game wins.

VARIATION 2: Instead of giving the puppets to the pupils, stand them in a lump of clay, or piece of Styrofoam. Ask the questions and give a signal. The first player to raise his hand and be recognized may pick the puppet he thinks answers the question. If he is correct, he may keep the puppet. If not, give the answer and return the puppet to the clay or foam. The player with the most puppets wins this game.

Bible Shake-up

PREPARATION: In the bottom of each section of an egg carton, mark a point value. You may either mark numbers 1 to 12 or choose two or three numbers (like 2, 3, and 4) and make several of each. Provide a small button or bean. Prepare a list of questions.

PLAYING THE GAME: Pupils may play as individuals or as teams. Ask a player a question. If he answers correctly, he may shake the egg carton vigorously. Open the lid to see where the button landed. This is the number of points the player earns for answering correctly.

If the player answers incorrectly, give the answer yourself and move to the next player. Plan to use the question later on.

VARIATION: Let the number system also be a means of determining which question to ask the player. In this case, use only a few numbers (2, 3, 4) rather than numbers 1 to 12. Prepare questions of varying difficulty to match your number system. Have the player shake the carton before you ask the question to determine which point group his question will come from. If he answers correctly, he earns that number of points.

Scrambled Eggs

PREPARATION: Print questions on small pieces of paper. Put each question in a plastic egg. (One good source of these is L'eggs hosiery.) Put the eggs in a box or basket.

PLAYING THE GAME: Let pupils play as individuals or in teams. Each time, the player must "scramble" the eggs before choosing one to take. He reads the question inside the egg. If he answers correctly, he may keep the egg. If not, he must return the question to the egg and the egg to the basket. The teacher should give the correct answer to the question so pupils can learn it. The player with the most eggs at the end of the game is the winner.

VARIATION: Instead of having pupils scramble their own eggs before answering a question, let the pupil who just played do this. The first time, the teacher will scramble the eggs and choose one. He will give it to the pupil to open and answer. When that pupil has answered (correctly or incorrectly) he will scramble the eggs and choose one for the next player. This variation gives the pupil a fun activity, even if he could not answer the question.

Bible Add-a-Word

PREPARATION: Type or write up a list of the Bible verses pupils have been using.

PLAYING THE GAME: Divide pupils into two teams. Give the first team a Bible reference. The first player on the team says the first word of the verse. The second player says the second word. The third player says the third word and so on. If the team has fewer pupils than there are words in the verse, begin again with the first pupil and keep going until the team has quoted the entire verse. They may continue until one player misses a word. Score 1 point for each word given in right order. If the team correctly quotes the whole verse, give an extra 5 bonus points.

If a team misses a word before they finish the verse, tell the rest of it to all the pupils. Lead them in saying the entire verse together. Then move to the second team, give them a reference, and continue the game.

One Last Word

Although you have discovered many different types of Bible games within these pages, no effort has been made to give an exhaustive list either of games to play or ways to play them. So—be creative. As you use these games and activities, you may soon discover other variations that your pupils will enjoy. Don't be afraid to experiment, for this is how new teaching ideas and methods are developed. But whatever you do, it is hoped that you, too, will discover for yourself the excitement of teaching with Bible games.